AF418855

THE SELF PUBLISHING CHECKLIST

5 STEPS TO GET FROM PAPER TO PRINT

NIKIEA REDMOND

Library of Congress Cataloging-in-Publication Data.
The Self-Publishing Checklist, Volume 1. Redmond, Nikiea.

Paperback ISBN: 979-8-9874573-0-6

Printed in the United States of America
by BCP Digital, KDP-Amazon & Lulu.

Edited by Victoria Kennedy
Cover Design with Canva Pro

For more tools, workshops and resources,
check out **www.nikiea.com**.

To my grandmother.
Thank you for bringing my mother into the world,
who brought me into the world. Thank you for inspiring my
passion to support writers becoming authors.
Forever grateful.

Table of Contents

The Self-Publishing Checklist is a tool for aspiring
authors sharing self-publishing advice and encouraging
you to make this one of your inspirational book
planning spaces; free from judgment and ready to hold
your ideas, mistakes, dreams and brainstorms from your
own research and life experiences.

Let's get your book out of your mind
and into the hands of your readers!

THE SELF PUBLISHING CHECKLIST

5 STEPS TO GET FROM PAPER TO PRINT

Start Where You Are

The "Self Publishing Checklist" is intended to support your writing to print journey. If you've just started and are writing a few notes here and there, this is for you too. In this book, you'll find the checklists and guides to track the progress as you work through what's needed to get you to the next step.

Get connected to your work. If writing your book is primarily for an extra source of income, own it. If writing your book is a lifelong passion to motivate others, own it. If writing a book feels like a calling that you're still figuring out the purpose of, own that too. Writing is the easy part for some of us. Yet getting the words to sound cohesive from your heart to your mind to paper is a skill that most writers take decades to master. In this journey of self-publishing, I'd encourage you to always seek help.

Whether it's paid, for hire help, bartered help or gifted help from a friend or family member; you will need someone or a group of someones in your corner to get this book done.

Getting started as a self-published author can be easier by guiding yourself with a monthly, quarterly and yearly timeline. Guiding your work through deadlines for sending your writing to the editor, hiring an illustrator, contacting a printer, and releasing your book are all ways to support the process of fulfilling your self-publishing checklist.

In this book, you'll find advice and tools to help you personalize your own self-publishing checklist with specific goals to complete your book project. Let's start visualizing your self-publishing process on the next few pages. Identify your self-publishing goals for the next 12 months starting today. Write down what it will take to get your goals done. Next create a checklist of what you need right now to get those goals accomplished.

- Here are good questions to start with:
- When do I want to start working on my book?
- If I need to hire an editor how long will they need?
- How much time do I need to complete my book cover design?
- When do I need to physically have my book?
- Am I hosting a book signing or book release?

We're starting where you are in this section of the book. It's important to know that you have a lot of the information you need already to finish your book.

THE SELF-PUBLISHING CHECKLIST

- Writing
- Editing
- Designing
- Printing
- Sharing/Selling

Self-Publishing Checklist

BOOK TITLE: _______________________________________

AUTHOR'S NAME: _______________________________________

☐ _______________________________________

Date Due

☐ _______________________________________

Date Due

☐ _______________________________________

Date Due

☐ _______________________________________

Date Due

☐ _______________________________________

Date Due

☐ _______________________________________

Date Due

☐ _______________________________________

Date Due

☐ _______________________________________

Date Due

☐ _______________________________________

Date Due

☐ _______________________________________

Date Due

2022 CALENDAR

January

MO	TU	WE	TH	FR	SA	SU
					1	2
3	4	5	6	7	8	9
10	11	12	13	14	15	16
17	18	19	20	21	22	23
24	25	26	27	28	29	30
31						

February

MO	TU	WE	TH	FR	SA	SU
	1	2	3	4	5	6
7	8	9	10	11	12	13
14	15	16	17	18	19	20
21	22	23	24	25	26	27
28						

March

MO	TU	WE	TH	FR	SA	SU
	1	2	3	4	5	6
7	8	9	10	11	12	13
14	15	16	17	18	19	20
21	22	23	24	25	26	27
28	29	30	31			

April

MO	TU	WE	TH	FR	SA	SU
				1	2	3
4	5	6	7	8	9	10
11	12	13	14	15	16	17
18	19	20	21	22	23	24
25	26	27	28	29	30	

May

MO	TU	WE	TH	FR	SA	SU
						1
2	3	4	5	6	7	8
9	10	11	12	13	14	15
16	17	18	19	20	21	22
23	24	25	26	27	28	29
30	31					

June

MO	TU	WE	TH	FR	SA	SU
		1	2	3	4	5
6	7	8	9	10	11	12
13	14	15	16	17	18	19
20	21	22	23	24	25	26
27	28	29	30			

July

MO	TU	WE	TH	FR	SA	SU
				1	2	3
4	5	6	7	8	9	10
11	12	13	14	15	16	17
18	19	20	21	22	23	24
25	26	27	28	29	30	31

August

MO	TU	WE	TH	FR	SA	SU
1	2	3	4	5	6	7
8	9	10	11	12	13	14
15	16	17	18	19	20	21
22	23	24	25	26	27	28
29	30	31				

September

MO	TU	WE	TH	FR	SA	SU
			1	2	3	4
5	6	7	8	9	10	11
12	13	14	15	16	17	18
19	20	21	22	23	24	25
26	27	28	29	30		

October

MO	TU	WE	TH	FR	SA	SU
					1	2
3	4	5	6	7	8	9
10	11	12	13	14	15	16
17	18	19	20	21	22	23
24	25	26	27	28	29	30
31						

November

MO	TU	WE	TH	FR	SA	SU
	1	2	3	4	5	6
7	8	9	10	11	12	13
14	15	16	17	18	19	20
21	22	23	24	25	26	27
28	29	30				

December

MO	TU	WE	TH	FR	SA	SU
			1	2	3	4
5	6	7	8	9	10	11
12	13	14	15	16	17	18
19	20	21	22	23	24	25
26	27	28	29	30	31	

2023 CALENDAR

January

MO	TU	WE	TH	FR	SA	SU
						1
2	3	4	5	6	7	8
9	10	11	12	13	14	15
16	17	18	19	20	21	22
23	24	25	26	27	28	29
30	31					

February

MO	TU	WE	TH	FR	SA	SU
		1	2	3	4	5
6	7	8	9	10	11	12
13	14	15	16	17	18	19
20	21	22	23	24	25	26
27	28					

March

MO	TU	WE	TH	FR	SA	SU
		1	2	3	4	5
6	7	8	9	10	11	12
13	14	15	16	17	18	19
20	21	22	23	24	25	26
27	28	29	30	31		

April

MO	TU	WE	TH	FR	SA	SU
					1	2
3	4	5	6	7	8	9
10	11	12	13	14	15	16
17	18	19	20	21	22	23
24	25	26	27	28	29	30

May

MO	TU	WE	TH	FR	SA	SU
1	2	3	4	5	6	7
8	9	10	11	12	13	14
15	16	17	18	19	20	21
22	23	24	25	26	27	28
29	30	31				

June

MO	TU	WE	TH	FR	SA	SU
			1	2	3	4
5	6	7	8	9	10	11
12	13	14	15	16	17	18
19	20	21	22	23	24	25
26	27	28	29	30		

July

MO	TU	WE	TH	FR	SA	SU
					1	2
3	4	5	6	7	8	9
10	11	12	13	14	15	16
17	18	19	20	21	22	23
24	25	26	27	28	29	30
31						

August

MO	TU	WE	TH	FR	SA	SU
	1	2	3	4	5	6
7	8	9	10	11	12	13
14	15	16	17	18	19	20
21	22	23	24	25	26	27
28	29	30	31			

September

MO	TU	WE	TH	FR	SA	SU
				1	2	3
4	5	6	7	8	9	10
11	12	13	14	15	16	17
18	19	20	21	22	23	24
25	26	27	28	29	30	

October

MO	TU	WE	TH	FR	SA	SU
						1
2	3	4	5	6	7	8
9	10	11	12	13	14	15
16	17	18	19	20	21	22
23	24	25	26	27	28	29
30	31					

November

MO	TU	WE	TH	FR	SA	SU
		1	2	3	4	5
6	7	8	9	10	11	12
13	14	15	16	17	18	19
20	21	22	23	24	25	26
27	28	29	30			

December

MO	TU	WE	TH	FR	SA	SU
				1	2	3
4	5	6	7	8	9	10
11	12	13	14	15	16	17
18	19	20	21	22	23	24
25	26	27	28	29	30	31

2024 CALENDAR

January

MO	TU	WE	TH	FR	SA	SU
1	2	3	4	5	6	7
8	9	10	11	12	13	14
15	16	17	18	19	20	21
22	23	24	25	26	27	28
29	30	31				

February

MO	TU	WE	TH	FR	SA	SU
			1	2	3	4
5	6	7	8	9	10	11
12	13	14	15	16	17	18
19	20	21	22	23	24	25
26	27	28	29			

March

MO	TU	WE	TH	FR	SA	SU
				1	2	3
4	5	6	7	8	9	10
11	12	13	14	15	16	17
18	19	20	21	22	23	24
25	26	27	28	29	30	31

April

MO	TU	WE	TH	FR	SA	SU
1	2	3	4	5	6	7
8	9	10	11	12	13	14
15	16	17	18	19	20	21
22	23	24	25	26	27	28
29	30					

May

MO	TU	WE	TH	FR	SA	SU
		1	2	3	4	5
6	7	8	9	10	11	12
13	14	15	16	17	18	19
20	21	22	23	24	25	26
27	28	29	30	31		

June

MO	TU	WE	TH	FR	SA	SU
					1	2
3	4	5	6	7	8	9
10	11	12	13	14	15	16
17	18	19	20	21	22	23
24	25	26	27	28	29	30

July

MO	TU	WE	TH	FR	SA	SU
1	2	3	4	5	6	7
8	9	10	11	12	13	14
15	16	17	18	19	20	21
22	23	24	25	26	27	28
29	30	31				

August

MO	TU	WE	TH	FR	SA	SU
			1	2	3	4
5	6	7	8	9	10	11
12	13	14	15	16	17	18
19	20	21	22	23	24	25
26	27	28	29	30	31	

September

MO	TU	WE	TH	FR	SA	SU
						1
2	3	4	5	6	7	8
9	10	11	12	13	14	15
16	17	18	19	20	21	22
23	24	25	26	27	28	29
30						

October

MO	TU	WE	TH	FR	SA	SU
	1	2	3	4	5	6
7	8	9	10	11	12	13
14	15	16	17	18	19	20
21	22	23	24	25	26	27
28	29	30	31			

November

MO	TU	WE	TH	FR	SA	SU
				1	2	3
4	5	6	7	8	9	10
11	12	13	14	15	16	17
18	19	20	21	22	23	24
25	26	27	28	29	30	

December

MO	TU	WE	TH	FR	SA	SU
						1
2	3	4	5	6	7	8
9	10	11	12	13	14	15
16	17	18	19	20	21	22
23	24	25	26	27	28	29
30	31					

"The idea is to write it so that people hear it and it slides through the brain and goes straight to the heart."

MAYA ANGELOU

Step 1

WRITING:
Trust Yourself, Trust the Process

Knowing the ins and outs of your story's message and overall theme is a valuable tactic to begin building your audience as a self published author.

Ask yourself:

- Who is my story for?
- How do I see it resonating with my audience?
- What topics will I reflect on at my first book talk?
- When is the best time for me to publish my book?
- Who will be on my team to help with getting this book completed?
- Which tools can I use to grow my reading audience?

The process in my experience of working with authors begins with having confidence in your story. Whether it's an informational book, children's book, fictional novel, photography book, memoir, coloring book, tutorial or art book; there's a back story of why you're writing or hiring someone to write your book. Since there are many challenges to overcome in the process of self-publishing, believing in your story will carry you through.

Technically, becoming a self-published author is opening a business. Your book is your product and you will be the primary force driving it's success and expanding it's readership. You have the power to create your book business the way you believe it will work for your lifestyle. Are you interested in publishing and sharing your book with primarily your close community? Are you interested in book talks? or hosting book clubs? Do you want to see your book on library shelves?

I'm sure right now, you're interested in getting this book done. And that's fine too. So what do you need to get started and get published? Here's the overall checklist to keep you on track.

Building your own checklist for self-publishing is important. The steps you need to take to complete your book will change depending on your book's goals. Also throughout the process you may choose to take a different route and that's okay. As long as you feel comfortable with your timeline.

FROM WRITER TO AUTHOR

For some authors writing is one of the longer stages of the book process. In my opinion, as an author you should give yourself time to write your story without feeling rushed. More than likely there are notes you've written over the years or a conversation you've had about your book. Try to collect everything you have to start writing your book.

Mixing up your writing space can also be helpful. Writing at the park, in a new coffee shop, at the bar, at a restaurant, at a bookstore, or in the library, Another way to mix up your writing is to put what you've written so far in the format of a printed book. Using tools similar to *Microsoft Word, GoogleDocs*, and sometimes *Canva* can help you format your book by:

- Title
- Copyright Information
- Dedication
- Table of Contents
- Introduction
- Chapters
- Acknowledgments
- About the Author

As an additional resource, this e-book includes a page-by-page template of a book's format at the end. The action behind moving from writer to author is execution. At some point you have to trust your story to be ready to be designed and printed.

Step 2

Edit, Edit, and Edit again

A great edit will always be the best decision for your book. In my experience, I find that it's easy for us to skip quality editing from an outside source. A different set of eyes that isn't your family or friend helps shape your story and make your message clear. The classics are still being edited. Remember that edits can happen when your book is published too and consider planning time to break from editing, pause for a few days or weeks. During that time you could start your book's design, to keep you on task for the print and publish deadline.

Editing Questions to Consider:

- How many weeks can I dedicate to reviewing my work?
- How long will it take the editor to complete their edits and discuss the changes I'd like to make?
- Who do I trust to read my book as is and provide honest feedback?

GETTING THROUGH WRITER'S BLOCK

Getting stuck happens. There are tools to help and professionals to hire to get you through it. To me, writer's block is a constipation of thoughts. At some point, after taking care of yourself, you'll release it and get back to your normal flow. Probably kind of a graphic definition but that's what it feels like.

Ultimately, this process of self-publishing is yours. If you decide to hire a writing coach or record your story with a voice capturing software or phone app and transcribe it; this is still your story.

When you feel stuck, taking a break is also a way to fuel your writing. Keeping published books near you helps with staying on track and visualizing your completed book. Trusting someone to read what you've written so far.

Whatever you decide to do, remember that this is your story, and you have the power to change it or keep it the same way you've written your story. Even the most legendary books are edited. Confidently step into this editing phase knowing you've done the best you can offer and believing in your story's message.

Step 3

Designing Your Book

Everybody knows what a book looks and feels like. Whether it's from a memory of your favorite children's book or a cringy feeling from thoughts of a statistics textbook. We've had many experiences with books in person and online. Most of the books you've read are designed intentionally to support the message of the story. From the cover to the copy to the placement of photos and illustrations. Now, as a self-published author, the design is governed by your choice.

You have the autonomy to create the visual representation of your book's message. Hiring support with this step could be a huge help in organizing your thoughts and increasing your capacity. A graphic designer who specializes in print media would be best to support your book's cover and copy design. There are also tools to DIY your book's design. CanvaPro and Adobe Spark are programs that offer templates for various book sizes.

Speaking of size, it's best to know the size of your book before starting this process. The size and the printer can determine how well the design flows. For example, if a printer you'd like to use to print your children's book only offers landscape printing at the 8.5 x 8.x5 size instead of the 7x9 size you were hoping for; you'll need to have the copy and cover redesigned to fit those margins accepted by the printer. Even before hiring an illustrator and graphic designer, you need to know what size your book will be. Many printers will send free copies of sample books from others to give you a better idea of their quality of printing.

BOOK DESIGN

Your book needs a full cover design, interior design or typesetting and book mockup design. These are the additional and essential components needed to print each book; other than your actual story or content.

DESIGNING YOUR COVER

Your book's cover is the face of your book brand. If you are on a tight budget you could try designing your book yourself with tools similar to Canva. Canva includes templates premade and fully editable under both their free and paid pro accounts.

If you have it in your budget, hiring a graphic designer, specifically a book designer is a great move. This level of support will allow you to make the space to create the style you visualize.

It's always best to ensure that photographs and art used to design your book cover are covered for commercial use. Check the photographs source to find the commercial use policy.

TYPESETTING YOUR COPY

Your book's copy or story and text also needs to be designed. This is generally called Typesetting. You can use tools like GoogleDocs or Microsoft Word to add page numbers and set up your books. These are all suggested sections to include in your book's layout for typesetting.

- Title page
- Copyright page
- Dedication
- Table of Contents
- Chapters
- About the Author page
- Acknowledgements

Step 4

Quality Production & Printing

If you'd like your book sold in bookstores and across different platforms, presentation and/or knowing the right people will get you on the shelf. You can design your book yourself using templates or hire a designer and illustrator to pull off your look. With either decision you make, be prepared to work long and hard at this part of your journey. It's one of the most essential steps. Imagine your book cover as the face of your story, CEO behind the company, you never see a CEO of a major company not up to par. Be sure to make an effort to create a book cover that is fully reflective of your story.

TIMELINE

It's helpful to know when you need the book printed to inform when you need to be finished editing and when design needs to start and when you need to send the book files to the printer so that your book arrives on time.

It's alway best to leave a cushion of a few days to a few weeks for all the steps in between writing and printing. Sometimes things come up for yourself or your team and you'll want to make sure there's room to take a serious look at your book at every step.

Here are good questions to start with:
- When do I need to physically have my book?
- Am I hosting a book signing or book release?

Types of Traditional Book Formats
- Paperback or Softcover
- Hardcover
- E-Book

CHOOSING AFFORDABLE PRINTING

The format and size of your book determine the cost of printing. Traditional sizes that generally print at a comparable price and accepted through most self-publishing platforms for online distribution:

- 6x9
- 5.5 x 8.5
- 8.5 x 8.5
- 8.5 x 11

CHOOSING PRINTERS

Printing is super important to consider ahead of time. The cost of your book should give you the freedom to charge prices that are comparable to what's out there already. Printing options ensure that your book is affordable enough to make a profit and stay competitive.

There are a few types of printing but the two I recommend for self-publishing authors are on-demand printing and bulk printing. On-demand printing is offered through companies like Lulu, Book Baby and KDP. This gives you the option to print smaller amounts of books at a good price. Bulk printing is specific for when you're ready to print about 200 or more books. Bulk printing is generally always the cheaper option because with books, the more you print the less cost from your pockets.

Local printers like BCP Digital are great options to use for printing. Local printers allow you to talk with an actual person and feel connected to the printing process. These types of printers generally send samples of their printed projects to you at no cost. Take your time and choose the best printer for your book. The printer can make all the difference for a great project.

Timeline
From Start to Finish

Step 5

SHARING YOUR BOOK:
Finding Your People

Writing can be challenging. Encourage yourself to take breaks. Even if you're holding the great news of your book for the "grand reveal", there are plenty of ways to begin building your tribe now. Your tribe is who will rock with you from start to finish, your new day ones, in a sense. Start now using your research, reposting quotes from pages with credit, posting photos from free sites such as Pexels that resonate with excerpts from your book or famous quotes. Remember to hashtag.

NETWORKING WITH AUTHORS

Authors love to support other authors. Learning about the publishing process through other authors is a win-win. Connecting with fellow authors for inspiration and to build your audience is one strategy to begin finding your "people". A few free resources to begin building a connection with your readers include but expand beyond this list below.

- Reddit
- Clubhouse
- Facebook, Instagram, Twitter, TikTok
- Social Clubs & Church Groups

WAYS TO SHARE YOUR STORY

Social media is a natural way to begin building your tribe of readers. Either through creating a separate profile as an author or book movement. Using hashtags is helpful to expand your visibility. Sometimes hashtags with smaller traction create more engagement. For example if the hashtag #inspirationalauthors has 1000+ posts it may allow for your post to be seen by more people actually following that hashtag. Yes, people really do follow hashtags, lol.

Aspiring authors who are artists can post artwork or photographs as content to start announcing your book's release soon. Maybe even resurfacing old art with a deeper storyline to pull in your audience in a different way than before. If you're writing a novel, memoir, or book of poetry; it may be helpful to record yourself handwriting a quote from your book or having someone take a photo of you holding your proof copy. Also making a reel about where you are in the process now.

THE RESEARCH

Writers read. It's a simple sentence with an essential impact on the self-publishing process. Read as much as you can to learn what's needed to speak to your audience. Audio books included.

CREATE YOUR PLATFORM

Start your own Ted Talk on your IG story, mail your own Media Kit to schools or bookstores and be in control of your strategy to expand your book's audience. Even if you hire professionals, being a Self-Published author is your business now.

Treat it like a mini LLC.

SHARING WITH THE WORLD

Amazon, Barnes & Noble, Good Reads are all examples of global platforms to connect readers to your book. As self-published authors, it's helpful to use these as tools to expand your brand and make your book accessible. Also, there is an ease in knowing these companies will handle your shipping and customer relations side of publishing your book.

There are a few challenges at times. The amount of royalties acquired through these platforms is at a lower rate than selling through your own website or social media accounts. Also gathering customer information to continue connecting isn't possible when using these options. One recommendation I have is to start advertising your book as a product sold on your website first. This way you can connect directly with the readers. As you build your audience you can publish with Amazon, Barnes & Noble, Good Reads to expand your reach.

A Note from the Author

Stay Inspired

You did it! You've started a major step in publishing your book, learning how to make this process easier. Congratulations on your journey! This is such a huge step in actualizing your goal to become a self-published author.

Publishing definitely doesn't have to be as hard as it was in 1997. I remember helping the first author I ever worked with pitch her poetry for the uhmteenth time to an out-of-state publisher assembling an anthology for poets and short storytellers. I remember we had been preparing a group of poems that we'd originally typed up from one of her poetry books. There were about 5 binders of poems typed by the electronic typewriter in her upstairs living room.

Poem after poem neatly sealed inside of plastic sleeves, safely kept by the binder's rings and sturdy exterior. Page after page, poem after poem waiting. Read aloud in her bedroom over and over. Recited to the *t*.

She always prepared her work for publishing. For her chance to see her name in shiny etched letters on a hard bristol covering the cover of her first book. She recited and recited. I felt every word as if she were a speaker in front of hundreds. At the most prestigious ball or author's gathering. She read to me like she was Maya Angelou reciting "and still I rise." Days and days, years and years. Those safely tucked away poems once imprinted on white paper now turned a tinge of cream. Her hands no longer typed the same words with vigor. Her mind could recite every word from poems of her own to "Haiwathas Daughter".

To make a full story short, she lived her life as I knew her believing, through story. Through words. Through poetry and prose. She was my grandmother. My first teacher on how to navigate this world of self-publishing. And she, like many other legends of my time have passed on without seeing her work published as her own. I'm sure she dreamt of writing and publishing since a little girl. I remember her stories about learning to read and dictate from a school debate club. She was one of two children her grandmother raised as an older woman. By that time she listened to the beauty of words through her grandmother's recount of bible stories and inspirational psalms.

My favorite story my grandmother never wrote was of her preparing for her first debate match. Her way with words always made me feel like I was there with her. Sitting in the woods next to a stream of water in Irmo, South Carolina probably around 1929. I believe my grandmother was about ten years old when she performed in her first debate competition. She used to carry her books with her all day to practice. She practiced in the woods so that she could hear her echo. She said it felt like she was already on stage. She used to practice reciting psalms and some of her favorite poems. I wish I could remember the one she told me she recited most. But I do remember her describing how quiet those woods were and I imagined her as she embraced that quiet and her voice strongly broke through. Preparing for her first competition.

My grandmother's stories will always live with the people she shared them with. Her way with words could move a room to feel her emotion. Yet over her lifetime. She hadn't published her own book. The steps to publishing were different 30 years ago. Even now some aspiring authors get lost in the process.

Over the years through countless hours of research, a lot of us have made the stride to take our idea from paper and pen to a printed book selling on Amazon, Barnes and Noble and beyond. This is no easy feat but I'm here to help.

Who are the ancestors who've touched your life and inspired you to write? Who inspires you to tell your story? How has that encouraged you to self-publish?

Resources

Advice on Writing From The Atlantic's Ta-Nehisi Coates by Emma Green, September 27, 2013.

Harriet Tubman Conductor of the Underground Railroad Serving Writers and Readers: African-American Literary Organizations by Diane Patrick, November 22, 2019.

23 Facebook Groups for Writers You Don't Want to Miss by Carson Kohler, March 29, 2021.

Advice From D. Watkins On How To Start Your Writing Career By Shantika Bhat And Kristiana Smith.

Dr. Koko's New Year Wisdom: Honoring The Past Is The Way To A Better Future By Kokahvah Zauditu-Selassie · Updated December 27, 2021.

Self-Publishing Resources can be also found at www.bcpdigital.com, BCP Digital is a legendary book printing company located in Maryland.

Thank you

Thank you to YOU for sharing this experience with me! To the Authors and Entrepreneurs that have trusted me over the last almost two decades. I am grateful to you.

Thank you to my mother Deitra Redmond and father Samuel Brown for bringing me into the world singing Luther Vandross. To my sisters Audra, Danielle and Kelli. To my Aunt Roxie, Uncle Larry, Uncle Radcliffe and Aunt Pam. To my A1, Day1, Reggie. To my cousins, especially my big cousin Lynette for keeping me focused and encouraged as a new Mommy. To my honorary kids Jordyn, Shay, Lil Raymont, Raven, Truth & Hari and the one I birthed, Ashton. To my Village (it's too many of y'all to fit on this page). To my brother Sam. To my aunts and uncles, nieces and nephews.

Thank you Ms. Victoria for editing this book.

Thank you to my ancestors for holding me down, letting me learn the lessons and paving my path. Especially my late grandmothers.

Thank you to my therapist for guiding me to a deeper healing.

Thank you to my Wings family. I wouldn't be who I am today without you. Kirsten and Scot thank you for being my rock.

To myself for pushing through loosing my sister Danielle in 2021, and the inner turbulence of going back home to start again raising my brilliant two year old. I did it! I'm so very proud of myself! I am my greatest treasure. Although this is my 2nd published book, it feels just a beautiful as the first.

2019 I PUBLISHED MY FIRST BOOK "INHALE DEEP"
AFTER A DECADE OF HELPING AUTHORS SELF-PUBLISH!
#EASTBALTIMOREBRED
THREE MONTHS CARRYING MY BABY BOY & VENDING
AT THE 'ABOVE IT ALL BALTIMORE' COMMUNITY EVENT
PHOTO CRED: MATT PRESTBURY, THE BLACK FATHERS FOUNDATION

Inella
1919-2016
DEDICATED TO THE 1ST ASPIRING AUTHOR I'VE KNOWN.
THANK YOU GRANDMA

NIKIEA REDMOND
SELF-PUBLISHING CONSULTANT

Nikiea Redmond has offered consulting services to self-published authors across the United States since 2009. Beginning as a book designer and learning the nuances of navigating publishing over the years has made it possible for her to support over 50 aspiring authors become self-published.

Today Nikiea is a Social Entrepreneur and Co-Director and Co-Producer of the award winning feature-length documentary *Anatomy of Wings*. Her entrepreneurship model specializes in providing self-publishing and marketing services to everyday people and non-profit organizations.

The Afro-American Newspaper presented Nikiea with the *Sam Lacy Award* for Youth Leadership in 2004. Nikiea is also a 2015 recipient of the *Black Wall Street Journal Award* for her Graphic Design work in Baltimore City. Redmond received her Bachelors in Corporate Communication from the University of Baltimore in 2011.

You can support Nikiea's work with authors at www.nikiea.com.

Join Nikiea at the next
"Get Published!" workshop visit
www.nikiea.com